Writing From The Source

Personal Writing As A Life Changing Practice

Linda Robson Bell

Robson Ryder Publishing
Suite 96/78 William Street
East Sydney NSW 2011

ISBN: 978-0-646-974-39-2

Self Help-Writing-Journaling

www.thewellspringcentre.com
info@thewellspringcentre.com

Acknowledgements

Every participant in every writing course and group I have run over the years. Each and every client I have spent time with. Your insights and honesty inspired me to write about just how deep and life changing personal writing can be. Petrea King, founder and CEO of the Quest for Life Foundation in Bundanoon, NSW. My daughter, Emma Franklin Bell for reading and offering ever-insightful feedback on this book and Robert who has supported my writing and my creativity over many, many years. Julia Cameron, author of The Artist's Way and a host of other beautifully written books on the power of writing and creativity. Authors too numerous to mention who have written about the joys, challenges and rewards of the act of writing.

Other Books by Linda Robson Bell

Bittersweet Short Stories - Ten Tales of Life, Love and Mortality

Dedication

To my family who help and support me always.

Dear Reader,

This is a book about writing. It's not about technique or plot or structure or writing a good sentence or any of the technical aspects of writing. It's about writing as a way of life. It's about writing as a:

- Soul nurturing exercise

- Path to self discovery

- Way to reduce stress and encourage a sense of calm

- Way to reflect on our lives

- Way to design a new future

- Spiritual practice

- Way to connect with our source

I call this Personal Writing - writing from the inside out.

My hope for this book is that it inspires you to write…and keep writing for the rest of your life.

And my hope for you is that writing feeds your soul and enriches your life

Best wishes, Linda

TABLE OF CONTENTS

Wellspring

*When you put your hand in a flowing stream,
you touch the last that has gone before and the first of what is still to come*

Leonardo Da Vinci

In the past, writing was only done by men in religious orders - the average person did not write. It kept a lot of power within that group but also meant that writing was associated with sacredness and the spiritual life. We live in a very different world now but I still believe that writing is a sacred act.

It connects us with our source, our creativity, our soul and as I like to think of it - our Wellspring - that bubbling source within us that makes us truly who we are yet is shared with all humanity. The quote above by Leonardo Da Vinci is a beautiful way of expressing that we are individuals but we are also connected to an eternally flowing stream.

A Wellspring is one of any number of metaphors for this precious part of us - our Vein of Gold, our Secret Garden, our Soul, our Creative Essence, our Inner Voice. I named my business Wellspring Centre because, for me, a Wellspring - a life-giving, healing, ever flowing spring of fresh water rising from within the earth is the perfect metaphor for our creative source.

As a child in England I was enchanted by the mysterious ancient stones, wells and springs that dotted the countryside. Springs bubbled up, as if by magic, from deep within the earth and flowed out, forming streams pools and rivers. This cool, clear water emerging from a mysterious hidden source below the surface fascinated me.

Many of these springs and wells were sacred and dedicated to saints. Long before Christianity came to England they were dedicated to Celtic goddesses and nature spirits. Many of them were known as healing places or shrines.

I see writing as a powerful yet easy way to heal, nurture and deepen our sacred relationship with our own Wellspring of wisdom, feeling, intuition, knowing, spirituality and love.

Whatever life offers us, gifts us, throws at us, challenges us with, amazes us with, almost crushes us with, puzzles us with and blesses us with - we can always write...

Introduction

A couple of years ago I started to feel restless, something was stirring in my soul. I sat with that feeling until this year when it gradually crystallized.

I want to write a book about writing.

This book is the result. So why now? We probably all sense that we are living through a revolution - the technology-information revolution. Our world is changing faster than many of us can keep pace with. At the same time it can feel like traditional values and beliefs and religious doctrines aren't keeping pace either. We may feel stressed by all this change, it can feel very unsettling and unpredictable. On the flip side, this is a very exciting time to be alive on this precious planet.

So, what does all this mean?

It means that in these super-fast, ever-changing times we also have a deep and powerful need to take some time to step out, step back, slow down and take stock. Time to just be rather than always coming, going and doing. Time to reflect, muse, remember, think and create.

I've found that one of the simplest yet most profound ways to do this is to write. When we write, especially by hand, we slow down and connect with a slower, more thoughtful life rhythm.

So this is my offering to you - my thoughts, ideas, reflections and learnings about the simple ways to weave Personal Writing into our daily lives, to open up to our creativity, to become more mindful and to clear the way for thoughts, ideas and insights.

Personal Writing, done regularly, becomes a writing practice and a writing practice is a spiritual practice. It takes us out of the everyday and connects us with something deeper, more profound - something transformational.

I recommend it to you…

PART ONE
PROCESS

Chapter One

The Desire to Write

The real voyage of discovery is not in seeking new landscapes but in having
new eyes
Marcel Proust

Do you feel restless?

Are you searching for something but you're not sure what? The quote above from the French writer Marcel Proust distils what this book about. You may want to *seek new landscapes* in your life but the voyage of true discovery is when we see our everyday world and our own lives through new eyes. We start to *see* in more depth, with more clarity, we discover what touches our spirit, what we find beautiful, what we *really, deeply* care about.

We become seekers and seers.

In this book we'll explore and discover what you feel passionate about, what you want to write about and how you can befriend and encourage the writer within you, that mysterious something that yearns to be heard - your unique creative voice and how that can be a true guide as you move forward with life.

On my own life adventure, both writing and reading have been my soulmates. They have fed me (literally, when I've earned money through writing and teaching), soothed me, nurtured me and expanded me. I can't imagine a life without writing and reading. Writing has given me gifts I'll treasure for the rest of my life and I want to share those with you.

This is not a book about writing techniques. This is a book about you and writing - that precious relationship - about how writing can help you live a life that is truly yours, that has depth and clarity reflecting who you know you really are.

In each chapter there are writing exercises that will help you explore writing and your relationship to writing, discover the creativity that lies inside you and expand your ideas, thoughts and feelings about writing and about your life path.

So Why Now?

At any time in our life we may find ourselves asking questions like:

- What have I done with the past decades?

- Am I really living the life I want to live?

- What's my true purpose in life?

- What am I going to do next?

- What do I feel passionate about and committed to?

- What is my life really about?

- When am I going to feel inner peace and calm?

Make the most of yourself by fanning the tiny, inner sparks of possibility into flames of achievement.

Golda Meir

Golda Meir was 71 years old in 1969 when she became Israeli Prime Minister. She was only the third woman in history to become a Prime Minister. In the volatile environment of the Middle East this woman dedicated her life to her beliefs. Whether you agree with her politics or not, she was a courageous woman who never wavered in her commitment to her deeply held values and to living a life she believed in.

Read her quote again to really appreciate its depth and meaning:

Make the most of yourself by fanning the tiny, inner sparks of possibility into flames of achievement.

It starts with trusting ourselves, with the idea that we create our own lives and that achievement starts small and grows. It doesn't matter where we start or how little writing we've done or how we feel about writing. Golda Meir reminds us that we need to *fan the tiny inner sparks of possibility...*

Many of us have deep doubts about how good we are at writing, how courageous we are or whether we have any writing talent. I can't count the number of times I've heard someone at the start of a writing course or workshop say: *'I'll just let you know that I'm no good at writing. I'm not creative.'*

This book's not about learning how to be a *good* writer. It's not about talent. It's about learning how to use the simple yet profoundly powerful act of writing to create a truly meaningful life for yourself.

Consistency

Anything we do consistently grows stronger and becomes more important to us and we become better and better at it until it becomes a habit. Writing is no different than anything else we do. If we exercise regularly and focus on becoming fit then we become stronger and exercising becomes more important in our life. We become better at it and we see the results.

If we focus on writing and make it an important and regular part of our daily life. It becomes a *writing practice*. Like a spiritual practice. And I believe it is a spiritual practice. If we consistently record our ideas, images, impressions, thoughts, experiences and discoveries, we will expand our creative self and come to know much more intimately who we are and what we want to do. In other words we'll start to get more and more clarity.

We will be able to notice what:

- Patterns emerge

- We focus on

- We think about

- We like and dislike

- Moves us

- We really care about

- Our true values are

We'll start to notice more and more about who we really are on a much deeper level.

If we don't write often then when we go back to it there's some unfamiliarity and we have to spend time catching up, getting back into it, getting used to it again. We may even feel we've lost some of our skill or inspiration. We usually haven't, we're just out of practice.

Like any spiritual practice, writers need to keep the writing practice up. It's not only about getting better it's about building up that solid relationship with writing so that we just can't imagine life without it. We nurture it and we work at it - like any other relationship we value.

What We Tell Ourselves, We Tell Our Cells

For years, for many of us, our creative selves may have been squashed, silenced, ignored or overlade with *stuff*.

There can be so much of this stuff that many of us tell ourselves and others that we're *just not creative* because we've lost touch with our creativity. But the truth is, it's still there - maybe buried, ignored or squashed down so that we no longer feel it or recognize it but it doesn't go away. It hides within us and whispers to us and sometimes we listen and sometimes we don't.

I've seen so many people create beautiful pieces of writing then often say: *Where did that come from?* They are stunned and amazed at what was inside them. For decades they've said to themselves:

- I'm not creative

- I can't draw, paint, write, sing etc etc

- I don't have a good imagination

- I'm not the artistic type

Have you said any of these to yourself? Or have you said any of these phrases to others about yourself? How often? What we're doing when we say these things to ourselves is that we're not only telling ourselves, we're also telling *our cells*.

Studies in neuroscience now show that when we think and say things to ourselves repeatedly they form neural pathways in our brains that become stronger and stronger each time we say them or even just think them. Once these pathways form it is more likely that we'll think and say these things again. This sets up a cycle. If you believe in manifestation, you'll know that whatever you think about you bring about. If you think you're not creative you're bringing that about in your life.

This cycle means we stop trying to express ourselves creatively. We literally scare ourselves out of trying. We've convinced ourselves and our cells that we won't be any good so we don't try.

Our Message

Somewhere inside us lies a message, a core central idea, a philosophy, a passion. I believe we all have it - a profound message we want to share. When we reach a certain stage of life and we've collected a host of experiences, we've lived millions of moments and we've taken in millions of messages – our brain, heart and spirit has reacted to these messages and, like distilling a fine wine or maturing a vintage cheese, we've ripened and we're ready to stop playing small and instead: *let our own light shine.*

Exercise:

Imagine this:

You've just won a nationwide contest.
The prize is that you get to write a book about your core message, what you truly, deeply believe in - just one book and it will be published, marketed and sold worldwide. It will be launched and placed front and centre in every bookshop,

everywhere. It will be given to every school student, college student, uni student. It will be put in every library.

Extracts will feature online, on social media and in newspapers and magazines worldwide. You have only one chance at this. You'll be interviewed on a host of media, TV, radio, podcasts etc.

Now this idea might fill you with passion and excitement or it might scare you. Note your response. There is no right or wrong, just note it. Then put that aside and do the exercise and see what you come up with.

The question is: What would you write about?

Really give this some thought and write down your answer. What *would* you write about?

That's the power of writing. It can help us find our core message - nurture it until it's ripe and ready and then we can choose to share it. Or not. We may not want to share our message - it may be too personal. But we can live it ourselves - every day. It can transform us.

In my years as a counselor and therapist and then my years writing and teaching, through hundreds of pages of jottings, hundreds of hours of listening and teaching and reading, I've worked out that my core message is:

Expressing Our Creativity Is What Makes Us Truly Ourselves And When We Do This We Can Contribute Powerfully To Creating A Better World

I believe out of that creative development comes everything that makes us human and connects us with everyone else, with the natural world and with the whole of creation.

Whatever you love and feel passionate about that's truly *yours*. It's the way you come to know who you really are, become more connected to the rest of humanity and at the same time more unique as an individual.

You differ from every other person on the planet and every other person who has ever lived or will ever live. Wow! And yet at the same time you are powerfully connected with every other person through your shared humanity.

Chapter Two

The Artist Within

Writing is the painting of the voice

Voltaire

Re-Discover, Re-Kindle And Re-Ignite

In the book, *Becoming a Life Change Artist*, Fred Mandell, Kathleen Jordan and Richard Leider showcase the lives and works of artists showing us that when we make life changes - we are artists working on the canvases of our own lives.

What happens to many of us is that our artist shows up in childhood but is gradually silenced by the voices of approaching adulthood and its responsibilities. A few people continue to work on their passion and become artists, with varying degrees of success, but most of us lose contact with that finger-painting, play-dough-molding, dancing, singing child who made up worlds in the living room or the adolescent who wrote long, unsent love poems or had plans to be the next rock star or best-selling novelist.

In later life we have done a lot, heard a lot, seen a lot, read a lot. This is the perfect time to tap into that part of ourselves that will give us true meaning now and in the future. To re-discover, re-kindle and re-ignite that passion. To bring back that artist within and bring her out of the wings and back onto centre stage.

Personal Renaissance

Psychologist and artist Ellen Langer in, *Being an Artist* writes about transforming ourselves by having what she calls a *personal renaissance* - a time in life defined by living in a way that gives our life purpose and meaning. What's so exciting about this is that it's a decision, we make a commitment - it's active. We're not waiting for things to change. We make the change. It doesn't mean we have to do anything extraordinary or need lots of money. We simply decide to live creatively and purposefully every day.

When you meet someone who's living this way you can feel how engaged they are with their life. It's not so much *what* they do, it's *how* they do it. They don't need to be doing anything amazing or dramatic (although they might be) it's that they bubble with life, purpose, passion. They do things they love doing. They're curious. They're open.

With writing, we can carve out and commit to creating a life that feels deeply meaningful for us and gives voice to that boundless creativity we all have inside us so that we can experience the delight of expressing ourselves, our dreams, our imaginings, our joys, our hopes, our trials, our poetry, our beauty, our offerings, our messages, our gifts, our words. We can create our very own *personal renaissance.*

Prepare To Be Amazed

Most of us have heard about people getting brilliant ideas in the shower or bath or just before falling asleep. So what's going on here?

At these times, when we're showering, bathing or drifting off to sleep we're usually:

- Relaxed

- Quiet

- Warm

- Often alone

- Not doing *external* activities

This creates the conditions for our mind to roam more freely yet at the same time be more focused. If we're alone soaking in a warm bath with relaxing music playing, lying back looking at the tiles on the bathroom wall, our left logical, daytime, organizing, planning brain can take a break and this allows our creative right brain to take centre stage.

We might think:

- What if…

- Maybe I could…

- I wish I could…

Images, memories, ideas, characters, stories, anything might just pop into our head in an amazing random burst of creative thought.

What we've actually done here without knowing it, is, we've set the scene where this is most likely to happen.

If we expect to pick up a pen or open up a computer file and just write, then sadly what we're doing is making it hard for ourselves.

We're expecting magic to happen but it often happens most easily when we set the scene.

Place

Some places just feel better for writing than others. But feeling like we're *only* able to write in a particular place that feels just right can also be a trap.

If you ever find yourself saying:

- I *need* quiet

- I *must* be alone

- I can *only* write in nature

- I can *only* write in coffee shops

- I *only* do good writing in my special journal

Warning bells!

If we say we can *only* write in certain places under certain conditions we can use this to put off writing.

I love to write when I'm alone with my favorite writing music on. I get really tempted when there are others at home to think, *I need to be alone to write* - it's so tempting. I have to stop myself and think instead, *I'd rather be alone and it's harder to write with people around but I'm going to write anyway.*

Exercise:

Take a few moments to think about your ideal writing conditions:

- Do you love being alone or with others?

- Do you like peace and quiet or do you prefer some noise and movement?

- Or does it depend on your mood or on what you're writing?

- What exactly gets you in the writing mood?

Now recall a place where you really loved writing or did some writing that you felt good about. Describe that place in detail.

Now read through your answers. What do your words tell you about where you really like to write?

This reveals to you your ideal writing place so that when the opportunity's there to create it - seize it and enjoy! And when it's - just write anyway.

Make it Easy on Yourself

It's been proven that rituals and habits help us get things done. I want you to discover what rituals or habits put you into your *writing zone*. We will each have different ways of doing this, there is no right or wrong way.

Make your ritual simple and, *only* use it for writing. Your mind will quickly associate your ritual with your writing time. Associations are very powerful. Even something as simple as using a particular pen that you only use for writing can help. When you pick up that pen your brain will go *Writing time!* In this way your mind is helping you break through procrastination and distraction instead of working against you.

But again, if you can't do this or it doesn't work for you - just write anyway.

Here are some suggestions:

- Have a special notebook that you use for your writing

- Light a particular scented candle that you use for writing

- Have a particular drink that you drink when writing

- Have two music tracks set aside for writing – one slow, one faster, depending on your mood.

- Sit in the same chair in the same spot

Things like a drink, a scent, a special chair, music etc. create a multi-sensory experience that your mind associates with writing. This makes it far more powerful and so it works far better than if we just grab a pen and notebook and tell ourselves it's time to get creative.

Exercise:

In your journal answer these questions now:

- When you're at home where do you feel happiest writing?

- Which room? Which chair? Or bed?

- If you're using paper, what notebook will you use?

- If you use a pen - which pen will you use?

- If you like fragrance - choose a candle or fragrant oil - which one?

- What food or drink makes you feel creative?

- Which music tracks will you select, one upbeat and one slow?

Treat your writing is a very special part of your life, which it is, so, when you can, make the doing of it as special as possible, but again, if that can't happen - write anyway.

So How do I Write?

Students often ask me - how do you write? Not physically, not pick up a pen and start, but:

- How do I write down what it is that's inside me?

- What is it that I really want to say?

Have you ever felt that there are ideas, theories thoughts, stories, memories, fantasies or poems that are sleeping inside you, just waiting to be woken up?

- But how do you actually do it?

- What's the secret?

There is no secret but there are some ways that make it easier to dive for those pearls, bring them to the surface and get them on the page.

Start, Right Here, Right Now

Freewriting

And it starts with what's called freewriting. Whether you've done freewriting before or not, that's OK, you can never do enough of it. I believe it to be the wellspring of a writer's life.

What's freewriting?

It's writing that's totally free - you just write, just write anything. The idea is to get any words on the page. If you can't think of anything to write, just right...

I don't know what to write, this feels awkward, stupid, boring, whatever. I don't know what to write. I want to write. This pen's really scratchy I need to

get another one. I like fountain pens. I remember my aunt used to use a
beautiful fountain pen with a gold nib......

Now you're on your way!

It's the opposite of school writing, business writing, uni writing any have-to writing. It's not results based. It just is. The only result we want is words on a page where there were none before - that's it.

Freewriting is where we get to know ourselves, rediscover ourselves and connect with ourselves. The act of putting pen to paper or finger to key and letting whatever flows through is truly liberating.

Freewriting:

- Opens the connection between our heart and the page

- Bypasses our rational brain that criticizes, orders, plans and judges

- Connects us to our inner self

It might start as a trickle or a gush. Who knows until you start. But nothing matters except starting and carrying on. Much of what you freewrite you'll never use. It doesn't matter. You can bin it, burn it, toss it or keep it!

But in the midst of your freewriting there will be gems! Little pools of insight, creativity, tenderness or brilliance!!

Many writers freewrite every time they sit down to write. It frees up their writing channel - gets the juices flowing ready for the *real* work of writing whatever it is they want to or have to write. When we see athletes or dancers before a performance - they warm up, they stretch and move, getting ready to perform. This is similar - writing freely - warming up, preparing, loosening up, stretching, getting into the flow.

Focused Freewriting

Often freewriting is writing about anything that comes into our mind and just going with the flow of thoughts as they arise. This is excellent but I have found that some people find this harder than having something to write about so this exercise focuses our mind on something to get the flow going.

If you find it easy to freewrite without a focus then do whatever feels good. It's always about getting the words out in the way that feels easiest for you.

Exercise:

Stop and relax. Take a slow deep breath and look around at where you are right now. Really look. If you're in a familiar place you'll see things that you don't really notice any more, that have become part of the scenery. But this time have a really good look.

Then focus on one thing. Study it in detail. Describe it in any way you like.

Write for five minutes without stopping. It's really important not to stop at all if you can do this. If you get stuck, write: *I don't know what to write* and then write the next thought that comes into your head and the next and the next...

Let's see how it works:

I'm looking at my favorite cushion it's blue and green and it reminds me of the ocean I bought it when I was on holiday in France in a little village near Marseilles. I remember the shop I bought it in it was painted white and really lovely and sold all these unusual cushions and other things for home. I love that cushion it's really old now what else do I think about my cushion, I don't know, what else is there to say about the cushion, it's a cushion a cushion, well it's not a pillow. I love my pillow, I hate hard pillows so last Xmas I bought myself a really thick soft pillow and I never realized how much it would affect my sleep......

See how it works! I haven't bothered about punctuation. This is the magic of freewriting.

In this exercise I've written about a particular thing so that there was a focus to my writing. And you can see how once you start, the first idea leads naturally into other ideas. This is why, in this exercise, we start by focusing on a familiar object because it breaks through any writer's block and gets us started and from there the freewriting gets a life of its own.

Don't think too much about what you're writing. Don't try and write well. Don't even think about punctuation, grammar, spelling. Just jot down your thoughts in a flow, a stream of thoughts onto the page or screen.

Free-flowing writing. This is what it is.

Chapter Three

Getting in the Flow: Mindfulness and Presence

Wherever you go. There you are.

(possibly) Confucius

A Clear Mind And An Open Heart

We tend to go through a lot of our life not *really* noticing what's around us. We are distracted or stressed or rushed and simply don't notice much anymore. Bringing mindfulness into our lives is one really good way of living a fuller life - the life of an artist.

Mindfulness means being present with a clear mind and an open heart. Otherwise we can move through life without really connecting - living on auto-pilot and missing out on wonder, enchantment and fun.

Being mindful connects us and engages us with our world. When we start to notice, we see opportunities for appreciation, wonder and curiosity everywhere. When we're mindful we see more and experience more even though the world hasn't changed. We notice finer and finer details and distinctions and what happens is that we start to get more ideas - we become more creative - because we are more open and curious.

Our busy lives can so easily and quickly throw us off track and we lose our mindfulness. We become distracted, overloaded and cut off from ourselves. Mindfulness is a simple quick way to get back to our centre whenever we notice we're feeling out of touch, frazzled, bored.

Again, stop for a second, look around, notice something - anything, and focus on it. Appreciate its shape, color, texture. You are now mindful. You are returning to yourself.

Remember, this is you in this life and this moment is one of your precious moments. Focus on your breathing, relax and slow it down, breathe into your abdomen, relax.

Ask yourself this:

- How does my body feel physically?

- Am I hot or cold or comfortable?

- Am I in pain or not?

- Am I relaxed or tense? If I have tension where is it in my body?

- What do my clothes feel like against your skin?

- Do I feel tired or energetic?

Make no judgment about these things just notice them.

This is the start of mindfulness.

Mindfulness allows us to approach the world with more childlike wonder, to play with new concepts, to see things from a shifted perspective. We can't always engage in new activities, but through mindfulness, we can look at the same things with fresh eyes.

Writing as Meditation

Writing can be a meditation. Meditation doesn't have to be something serious that requires study, the meditation needed for writing can be very simple. It's about being calm, relaxed and focused on our writing and nothing else.

With mindfulness meditation our intention is to be mindful, that is, to be aware of what is going on in the present moment. Often the breath is used to anchor us in the present moment in mindfulness meditation.

It can be as simple as sitting still and taking a few long slow breaths. Then bring your awareness into the present. Notice where you are. Notice your body on the chair.

Whatever thoughts, distractions, sounds, images, ideas, or feelings arise - nothing is excluded. We simply pay attention to whatever is there. We do not judge or evaluate. Whatever happens, whatever occurs is okay - we just sit quietly and observe.

The Sanskrit word *shamatha* means peaceful abiding. Peaceful abiding is a lovely description of mindfulness. It is steady and calm like the anchor holding a boat in rough water. The boat bobs up and down, the rope to the anchor shudders and pulls but if the anchor is placed in the right way it stays firm, embedded in the earth below the windblown and ruffled surface.

The goal of *shamatha* practice is to become aware of awareness. When we practice mindfulness and awareness we feel more solid. The winds of emotion may still blow, but instead of being ruffled or even swept away, we hold still and notice, we may say to ourselves: *I'm feeling stressed, annoyed, overwhelmed and this is how it is and I accept it.* When we become aware, then accept, we allow a core of calm to exist in our centre and the more we practice mindfulness, awareness and acceptance, the more this calm centre grows.

Solitude

To start creative work - to allow that first trickle - we often need some solitude so that we can:

be by ourselves and with ourselves so that we can be ourselves

Alone and quiet, moving the pen across the paper is meditative. Tap, tap, tapping away on a keyboard is meditative. If you write in a quiet place, the very act of writing can draw you deeper into your centre. Often when we write for a while we find that the pen takes on a life of its own as it moves swiftly across the page pouring out what we want to say. A piece of paper will never judge you, hurry you, belittle you.

Noticing

Great writers are great noticers. They observe and draw our attention to what is around us that many of us haven't noticed or we noticed once and over time we just don't notice anymore.

Noticing is a simple way to become more mindful and creative. To pay more attention, to observe, to notice.

That's why it's helpful to carry a small notebook in your bag or use notes on your phone and when you hear or notice something you can jot it down, there and then in the moment. It will be lost otherwise. Writing down observations regularly alerts our mind and we start to notice more than we did before.

You can notice and write down:

- Your thoughts and actions
- Other people's words and actions
- Things that catch your eye
- Mundane things you don't usually pay any attention to
- Anything that touches you emotionally

- Ideas and images that visit your imagination

- Details about anything

We don't, of course, want to notice *everything*. Our brains filter out most stuff or we wouldn't be able to cope but what we can do is pay more attention to what we *choose* to notice. We can focus on what makes our lives richer and more meaningful and notice less those things that we don't want in our lives.

A popular artist's quote is: *You don't see in order to draw, you draw in order to see.*
The same can be said for writers. *We don't think and see in order to write, we write in order to think and see.*
Leonardo Da Vinci used the phrase: *saper vedere* meaning *to know how to see.* This is what writers and artists do, they know how to see.

Exercise:

Cloud Gazing

Have you ever looked up at the clouds and thought about what they look like? If not, or if you haven't done this for a long time, maybe since you were a child, go and have a look right now. Get a piece of paper and a pen. Go outside now or go to a window and look at the clouds.

- Do they remind you of anything?

- Do they look like something? If so, what do they look like?

- Do they make you think about anything?

- What do you feel looking at these clouds?

Write down your thoughts and feelings. Sketch the clouds if you like. Jot down words that come into your mind? Don't stop yourself. Whatever words you think of, write them down, freewrite them - poetic words, whimsical words, funny words, weird words, childish words or boring words. Whatever comes into your mind. If this brings back memories of cloud gazing as a child, freewrite about that. If you get an idea for a story or a poem - start writing that. Don't think about it - just write.

Flow

Writing brings us into the now. When we're writing we are immersed in the present moment, in what we are writing. Either typing on a keyboard or writing with a pen on paper we have a direct, present relationship with what we're doing.

Over 40 years ago Mihaly Csikszentmihalyi began studying *flow states* - the state we're in when we're totally engaged. It's that feeling we have when we lose ourselves in what we're doing - time passes without us noticing. We are not thinking about anything except what we are doing. We are totally present. This is when writers say they do their best writing.

Sometimes in this state writers can feel they've been visited by the muse or the writing is just coming into them from somewhere and they are writing it down. In the midst of this state we want to carry on with what we're doing no matter what and for as long as we can.

We lose that self-conscious and self-critical part of us that is the biggest foe of writing, that stops us being creative. If we can get past that initial resistance and lose ourselves in our writing that's when we feel the pure joy of it.

Past and future recede, worries and frustrations recede. We are just there - ourselves and our writing. Nothing else. This is flow.

People have said that when they're in a flow state they:

- Have no fear of failure

- Are not thinking about what others will say or think

- Don't feel frustrated

- Feel like the writing is flowing through them

- Feel visited by the muse

- Feel happy and fulfilled

- Don't want it to end

- Feel deeply creative

- Feel connected to something bigger than themselves

- Sense a spiritual connection

Distractions are the enemy of flow so we need to make it as easy as possible to get into and stay in a flow state. It is said to take about 15 minutes to get into. So what does this mean for your writing?

Translating this into useful, practical terms means we need to give ourselves about 15 minutes to get into our writing and we need to cut out distractions if possible.

What we're talking about here is the ideal state and we can find it very hard or almost impossible to reach very often. Maybe we never reach it. When it's not on offer we still write.

Chapter Four

Awaken Your Creative Spirit

*Concentrate the mind so that you can study not from books, but from
observation, which is the first awakening of the soul
Satguru Sivaya Subramuniyaswami, Hindu mystic*

The Creative Process

As a species, we create beyond what is instinctive and beyond
what is needed for mere survival. Creativity is a gift our species
has been given. If we nurture and develop our creativity we are
changed forever.

When we start writing or start writing something new or play
with our curiosity or have fun with our writing it's so important
not to judge what we write. Our culture is competitive. Healthy
competition can be positive but it is a problem when it leads to
judgment while we're exploring, learning or trying out new ideas.

We need to be curious, play and try things out. Just play with our
creativity or explore it to deepen and enrich our lives. We need to
be able to experiment, to just *be creative* and not worry about the

41

results, whether we think what we produce is *good* or *bad* or whether we have talent or not.

When we've created and we move to ordering, editing and polishing our writing there is a place for deciding what we like and don't like. What we feel works. What we want to keep and what we want to toss out. But that time is not during the creative process. During the creative process the focus is on just creating.

Tip:

Apart from your journals or writing notebooks or computer files, get yourself a small, unlined notebook to carry with you. Doodle. Sketch. Being 'good at drawing' is irrelevant. This is about noticing and recording ideas, impressions, thoughts and opinions in both words and symbols.

How Does It Work?

In our society the left brain (as we usually call it) dominates. This is the side of our brain that plans, orders, organizes, works things out, makes decision and solves problems. Without all these elements, we wouldn't have a society that works for us.

However...

Our lives can become dominated by our left brain functions leaving less and less time or space for us to use our right brain. This is the land of our imagination, it's where we have outrageous and beautiful ideas, flights of fancy and grand visions. This part of our brain doesn't use words and logic it uses images.

The danger with the left brain for writers is that it likes to play safe. It will stamp on ideas that it sees as outside its safety zone, outside what fits in with what it already knows, that don't make sense to it.

To tap into our creativity to its fullest we need to break through these reactions somehow and come to embrace our right brain as our wellspring of creativity. We don't have to accept everything we come up with but we need to try not to reject things that challenge our preconceived ideas, seem out of left field, whacky, weird, over-the-top, stupid or childish.

Our right brain makes associations that often don't follow what our ordered left brain would come up with and often feel nonsensical. Like the associations we have when we dream - our right brain doesn't know about what's *supposed* to go together. It's free-flowing, free-ranging, imaginative and whimsical and wonderful

It might conjure up blue trees or snakes with feathers or …

Writers use both sides of the brain. The right brain to get new and original ideas, see images, make things up, make connections, use metaphors, have flights of fancy and our left brains order, plan, decide and edit our scribbling.

When people say they're *not creative* what they often mean is, they spend so much time using their left brain functions they simply don't access the images and ideas that come into their right brains or if they do they dismiss them straightaway.

So we first need to notice when we get creative ideas that pop up spontaneously. We often reject them or they're crowded out by the mass of left brain thoughts about catching the bus, paying the bills or ringing the dentist.

Griffins And Walking Sticks

I just love mythical animals like dragons and griffins. One day this idea arrived in my head about a man who has a griffin. Then another character just seemed to arrive - a woman with a bright pink walking stick. I jotted these down and started writing. What developed was a short story about a woman with a pink walking stick who kept a griffin as a pet. She met a man in a café and gave him a griffin's egg.

After I'd worked on this story for a while I sent it off and it was published. I could easily have dismissed those first ideas that came to me or not even really noticed them but because I've practiced taking notice of these ideas and writing them down I captured them at the time. They are often our most precious ideas - our most creative. Treasure them. Nurture them. Polish them. They truly are gems of our creative self.

Stifled Creativity

Our creative self is that precious part that is uniquely *us* and makes us different from *everyone else who has ever lived or will ever live*. When we write regularly and strengthen our writer's voice, we forge a deeper bond with that creative self that is ever-changing yet always stays uniquely us.

Julia Cameron in her book *Vein of Gold* talks about the sadness people can feel from: *The bottled up wish for a more magical life…* bottled up creativity, stifled by the responsibilities of life and the expectations of others, creativity that was squashed or even belittled when they were young.

Do you ever find yourself pining for something more than the everyday? Do you crave for a return to the enchantment we felt as children when a shell or a petal was the most glorious and fascinating thing we'd every found? Where sunlight glittering between the leaves of a tree seemed like magic?

As adults it's so easy to feel like we've lost that sense of wonder that is so much a part of creativity, but… it's not lost, it's still there. In a special place where that magical life still lives.

When we rekindle and reconnect with that creative child we often feel emotional, it often feels bittersweet - sad but also beautiful, touching, nostalgic and we want more of it. And we can have more of it, it hasn't gone anywhere, it's just been forgotten or silenced or ignored. But it doesn't have to be any more.

Our Inner Child

What childlike pleasures did you enjoy in the past that you don't do any more or hardly ever?

- Building sandcastles
- Drawing with fluoro textas

- Doing cartwheels

- Playing with play dough

- Reading Roald Dahl or Harry Potter

- Watching kid's movies or TV shows

- Bouncing on the trampoline

- Buying and eating doughnuts with faces on them

- Writing silly rhyming poems

Try doing one of these without making an excuse - just for the fun of it, just because you want to.

No creative work has ever yet come to birth without play

Carl Jung

Chapter Five

Finding Your Writer's Voice

Words are the voice of the heart

Confucius

Writer's Block - The Stifled Voice

Many of us have a desire to write but then come up against so-called writer's block - we just can't write anything or we write a little and then get stuck, think what we've written is not good enough. Then we give up.

I've read a lot about writer's block being a fear of the blank page and not knowing how to get started. I think it's deeper than that. I think it's our fear of not knowing what we have inside us and how creative we might be if we let ourselves go. I think coming face to face with ourselves and our words there in front of us scares us and stops many of us from even starting and makes many of us give up very soon after.

Earlier I suggested freewriting to break through this fear-based block. By doing this, we start to develop a fantastic sense of freedom to explore, ask questions, make mistakes, discover our creativity and blossom. To be truly us!

When we try writing and our first attempts are not great, in fact they may be really unpolished, we then might think that we've proved to ourselves that we're not very good at writing, that we're not creative and we shouldn't have tried. But our early attempts, no matter how crude, are a normal stage in the creative process that nearly everyone goes through. Instead of putting ourselves down, we need to celebrate the fact that we've written something, anything!

In every workshop and class I have run we would look at this fear of writing and I would ask participants what scared them most about writing. This is what they shared with me - what they were frightened of:

- Being exposed - showing ourselves to the world. 'Appearing naked on TV' as one student put it

- Being judged, ridiculed or criticized

- Getting it wrong

- Looking stupid

- Not being any good

- Being really good

- My family, friends, workmates might read what I've written and be shocked, embarrassed, will laugh or criticize

- People knowing what I really think and feel

- People not liking me

- People being shocked or disappointed at who I really am

- Being shocked or embarrassed about my ideas and what I'm writing about

- Finding out that I am creative

These reveal to us that much of our fear is about other people reading and judging our writing. One way to move through this is to write and not share it with others. Often if we keep writing just for ourselves, at some stage we will feel drawn to share some of our work with others. Or we may never want to. Because we don't have to share our work with others if we don't wish to, we can move forward at our own pace as we build confidence in our unique and beautiful writer's voice.

Exercise:

If you still feel blocked with your writing, if you procrastinate then freewrite about this right now:

- What scares me about writing? Write as many things as you think of as quickly as possible. Be as honest as you can no matter how silly it sounds. If you can't think of anything to write then ask yourself this question:

- If I have no fear of writing - why aren't I writing?

- Why haven't I written the book, memoir, poetry, play, article, kept a journal - whatever is in my heart that I yearn to write?

Jot down your answers as quickly as possible.

Now read what you have written.

- What do your answers reveal?

- Do they reveal anything surprising?

- What are your reactions to your answers?

I would then ask participants:

If writing's that scary then why do you still do it or still want to do it?

Every time I asked them this, their answers would always include:

- I want people to know what I think

- I want to know what I think

- I want to create

- I want to share my knowledge

- I want to inform, entertain or move people

- It makes me feel good

- It soothes me

- It brings me closer to myself

- It's like a meditation

- It's spiritual

- I couldn't live without it

- I feel powerful when I write

- I want to be good at it

- I want to be published

- I want to be famous

- I want to make money

- I want to help people

This showed that even though they were fearful about sharing their work, on some level they wanted to share, to have others read what they'd written.

However, it often isn't only others we might be concerned about. Many of us are skilled at judging ourselves and undermining our own worth and work. One way to start changing your beliefs about yourself, your creativity and your writing ability is to notice anything negative that you think or say about yourself. Notice when you have doubts about your ability or you criticize your desire to be creative.

Notice if you think things like:

- Who am I to....?

- I won't be any good so why start?

- I've left it too late

- I don't know what to write

- I'm too tired

- I can't be bothered

- I'm too busy

- I'm wasting my time

- It'd be better to......

- It's too hard

Every single time you say something like one of these to yourself, replace it instantly with something that nurtures and encourages you. Reword these limiting thoughts with positive and uplifting thoughts.

Something like:

- I'm starting to explore my creativity

- I'm starting to get used to writing

- I'm discovering writing as a part of my life

- I'm just going to have a go anyway

- I'm going to have some fun

Although we probably don't consciously realize it, many of us are actually afraid of our creativity, our potential and our power so we dampen down that part of us and keep it locked away and don't share it with anyone. But is that what we really want to do? When we are truly honest with ourselves. I don't believe it is.

Giving Voice To Our Words

Just as we all have a speaking voice and a singing voice, we all have a writing voice. Your unique and individual way of seeing things. When you first write you might think you don't have a voice - but you do. We all have a writer's voice. It's unique to you like your speaking voice or your fingerprint or - everything about you.

Your writer's voice might start as a whisper. Very small, very quiet - almost unnoticeable. Or it may be bold and loud -

whatever it is, treasure it, nurture. Don't be afraid of it. Don't discount it. Just keep expressing it.

The more we write, the stronger our writer's voice becomes, it speaks rather than whispers. At first you might think your writing's not great and your writer's voice is boring, or clumsy or - whatever - or you might think it's beautiful, sensitive or funny or brash. It's all fine.

Over time as you write more and more often you'll sense how a certain style is emerging, that you have a certain way of seeing the world, of speaking to yourself or others from the page, a certain way of expressing yourself, of using certain words or phrases. This is your writer's voice emerging.

The very best way to develop your writer's voice and deepen your writing is to write from your heart then gradually you'll find your own true voice. It'll grow louder and stronger the more writing you do, it'll develop and refine with practice and become more you.

Letting Ourselves Get It Wrong

Mistakes are the portals of discovery

James Joyce

Without even realizing it most of us evaluate the creative efforts of others. We don't usually question this. We have critics, we have reviewers, we discuss whether we liked a book or film or a performance or an artwork. I think there's a place for evaluation or we would never have excellence.

But when we are starting out or writing for pleasure or just being creative let's put evaluation on hold. This is not easy for most of us. We will still tend to judge our first attempts at writing something even if we try not to.

When we're experimenting or trying things out we need to be free to make mistakes, fail and to just write anything and not worry about the quality.

Sometimes when we write stuff and read it back, it makes us cringe, laugh, blush or feel irritated or disappointed because we think it's boring, clumsy, not saying what we were trying to say - whatever. Then we might feel like giving up, we might think that this proves we will never be able to write well.

We need to move through this. If we don't, it will rob us of untold pleasure and before we know it we will have lost years or decades when we could have enjoyed being creative.

When we're evaluating our early efforts it's as if we're critiquing a professional writer or an edited piece of writing. The truth is we hardly ever get to see the early, raw attempts of professional or experienced writers. What we see is the polished, edited, reworked version. Published writing is always edited and refined. That's the process of bringing any creative work to fruition.

Instead of thinking that writing that doesn't please us proves that we aren't any good at writing and we'll never be as good as we want to be, we need instead to feel good that we've actually written and only then choose what to do with it. We can:

- Use it as a starting point for developing something better

- Toss it

- Burn it

- Laugh at it

- Keep it to look back on and see how much we've progressed.

- Keep it, rewrite parts of it, polish it and edit it

- Whatever - just try not to get upset about it

Most great writers have got to where they are by throwing out a lot of stuff.

You don't have to even read what you've written if you don't want to. Put your writing away and look at it later. As you write more, your curiosity will probably outweigh your fear and you'll read what you've written.

When you've written something you're really not happy with don't judge it, instead ask questions. This will open up your process rather than close it down. Through this you can learn and become better.

Rather than judge, ask yourself:

- What do I like in this writing? What works?

- What do I like about which parts?

- What am I not satisfied with in this?

- What doesn't work?

Objectively assess your writing.

- How could it be written better?

- If I'd written this in a way that I would have been happy with what would I have written?

You can use your answers to do more work on it. Write it differently. Or rewrite it.

When the poet Robert Frost wrote poems that he didn't think were good enough he simply labeled them *exercises* and his expectation of them being *poems* was changed. Then he felt OK about them and may have used them for ideas. Mistakes make us feel like we've failed. If we rename what we're doing as exercises or experiments we can be much more loving and accepting of ourselves and in the end the rewards will surprise us.

At other times what you write might surprise you with its freshness and creativity and you'll wonder how you could have written it and you'll wonder where it came from.

This is when you're discovering your creative self! You're getting a glimpse of your very own creative magic!

Chapter Six

Our Senses - Doors and Windows to Our World

The world is full of magic things patiently waiting for our senses to grow sharper

W B Yeats

Our Physical Senses

We have five physical senses and many think at least one other - our *sixth sense* and maybe more. Most of the time we don't think about them until something interferes with their smooth running.

Every second of every day we are immersed in our senses. We are seeing, hearing, touching, smelling and tasting all the time. As children we lived in the moment and reveled in our senses. We used them to discover the endlessly fascinating world around us.

But gradually, over time, we become dulled to our senses and we don't really notice, we just take in a vast array of things. Also because we see a lot of things every day we become so used to them we don't really notice them anymore.

As humans we rely mainly on sight to appreciate and understand our world and with the rise of technology this is even more so. Apart from when we might close our eyes during the day, we are looking all the time we're awake. But do we really *see*?

In Chapter Three, *Getting in the Flow* I talked about noticing. It really is crucial in developing a deep and satisfying writing practice, to notice. To somehow break the spell of familiarity and see things again through new eyes. It's quite simple to do and it's just about getting into the habit of doing it.

The second sense we rely on most is our hearing but again we become so used to sounds that we hear all the time that we don't really notice them. Those of us who live in cities live in a 'surround sound' environment often day and night. We often don't really experience much silence.

I noticed this recently. I live in the middle of a big city, Sydney, Australia. Where I actually live is not on the street front and is quiet, especially at night. But - I visited a friend in the country recently and stood outside on her verandah in the early morning and I noticed it was almost totally silent. I had thought where I lived was quiet until I stood there. Now and again I heard a bird or the faint rustling of leaves, otherwise it was as close to silent as I had experienced in a long time.

As I settled I found myself taking long, slow, deep breaths, taking in the still cool air and all I wanted to listen to, was the quiet. I felt relaxed and as if I was reconnecting with life. It was a beautiful and sacred time with myself and with life.

Then there are smell, touch and taste. These are seen by many people as secondary senses to seeing and hearing but what's really fascinating is that it's been shown that a smell can trigger a memory and return us to former time more quickly and powerfully than any other sense.

This may be because our sense of smell is very primitive and primitive senses and drives are very immediate and powerful. They are deeply embedded in the oldest part of our brain and they developed from our need to survive in the wild. To be able to smell a forest fire, an animal or smell the rain coming, long before it happened was vital for us. So we are deeply connected to our senses in a very primal and ancient way.

What's fascinating is that when we use sensory words to describe something, we conjure it up in our imagination and our body and feelings respond to it as if we are really doing that thing.

This is at the heart of fiction writing, poetry, storytelling, advertising and the power of visualization. A good writer works on our imagination so that we see, hear, smell, taste and feel as if what's being described is real and we are there. That's the skill of top writers and poets such as:

Charles Dickens - Extracts From: *A Christmas Carol*

 "…not a squeak and scuffle from the mice behind the paneling, not a drip from the half-thawed water-spout in the dull yard behind, not a sigh among the leafless boughs of one despondent poplar…"

"…ancient walks among the woods, and pleasant shufflings ankle deep through withered leaves…"

"Nor was it that the figs were moist and pulpy, or that the French plums blushed in modest tartness from their highly-decorated boxes…"

Christina Rossetti - Extract form Verse 1: Goblin Market

Morning and evening

Maids heard the goblins cry:

"Come buy our orchard fruits...

Our grapes fresh from the vine,

Pomegranates full and fine,

Dates and sharp bullaces,

Rare pears and greengages,

Damsons and bilberries,

Taste them and try:

Currants and gooseberries,

Bright-fire-like barberries,

Figs to fill your mouth,

Citrons from the South,

Sweet to tongue and sound to eye;

Come buy, come buy."

George Orwell - Extract from: *1984*

"Outside, even through the shut window-pane, the world looked old. Down in the street little eddies of wind were whirling dust and torn paper into spirals,

and though the sun was shining and the sky a harsh blue, there seemed to be no color in anything, except the posters that were plastered everywhere."

Coming To Your Senses:

As Petrea King of the *Quest for Life Centre* says, we need to *come to our senses.* A commonly used phrase but do we stop to think about what it is really saying? We need to ground ourselves, to come back to what our senses are telling us and listen to them.

One really powerful, fun and easy way to have something to write about or to be able to break through writing blocks is to use our senses as a starting point.

A really simple writing exercise is to choose one of the senses and write a piece using *just that one* sense as the reference point.

Exercise:

1. Look away from this page for a moment and concentrate on what you can see. Choose something from what you see. Really study it. Describe it in detail. Write down all the visual details - color, size, shape etc

2. Listen. Stop reading this book and listen. Really listen. What sounds can you hear? It is rarely ever completely silent so what can you hear? Write about what you can hear right now.

3. Move your tongue around your mouth – what can you taste? This can be tricky if you haven't just eaten or

drunk. Just concentrate. What is the taste? Write it down. Write about what you can taste right now.

4. Breathe slowly and deeply through your nostrils. What do you smell? What exactly is it? Describe it in words. Write about what you can smell right now.

5. Focus on your body now. What touch sensations are you experiencing right now? What do your clothes feels like? Is the air touching your skin warm, cool, humid? Is your body comfortable in the chair, on the bed or wherever you are? Write down what your sense of touch is telling you right now.

When you've done this exercise you'll realize just how much is going on every second of every day. This is the stuff of good writing. Noticing the sensory experiences you are going through, using all the senses.

We can also imagine the sensory experience that others are going through. This is what fiction writers and journalists do. We can also remember the sensory experience we've gone through in the past. This is what memoir writers do.

When you've done this exercise you'll have *come to your senses* and you can go back to them whenever you need or want to.

Exercise:

Focusing on just one sense

1. Choose a meal time when you can eat alone. Focus on the *smell* of the food as you eat. Really savor it. When you've finished, start to write. Write about that meal, solely focusing on what you *smelled* rather than what you tasted. Taste will be the most prominent when it comes to food but focus instead, this time, on smell.

   - Describe what your food smelled like and what you did to experience that - did you inhale the steam rising from the food? Or did you do something else?

   - How did the fragrance of the food affect your enjoyment of it?

   - Did the smell and taste of the food differ?

   - How did you experience the smell? In your nose? Did it make your eyes water?

   - Was the food strong smelling or mild?

   - Which scents were prominent in the meal?

   Go into great detail about the smells, really describe them and compare them with other foods or other experiences of this food. Stay sensory, try not to veer off into visual description or factual commentary about the food.

2. Go for a walk and focus on *sounds*. You are hearing something every step of the way but often we don't notice.

    - What do you hear as soon as you step outside?

    - Then what do you hear, then what do you hear?

    Take a break regularly and jot down notes about your experience of hearing in as much detail as possible.

3. Take a trip in a bus, train, car, ferry or on a bike. You will hear, see, smell and taste things but concentrate on what you *feel* through your skin.

    - What do you feel touching your skin?

    - Are you hot or cold or comfortable?

    - What do the different parts of your body feel like?

    - How does your face feel? Your hands? Your feet? Your back? Your ears? Your feet?

4. Drink a glass of water. Focus your attention on the *taste*. We tend to think that water has no taste but it usually does. It can be very subtle. But water tastes different in different areas. It can even carry the residual taste of the container. Focus on describing in detail that faint taste. What is it exactly? Write down what you experience.

5. Pick something you can *see*. Now study it and describe its color or colors. Nothing else *just the color*. What color is it, exactly? Say it's yellow for example.

   - What kind of yellow?

   - *Exactly* what kind of yellow?

   - Is it a green-tinged yellow or an orange-tinged yellow?

   - Or something else?

   - What does this yellow look like - egg yolk? Lemon? The sun? A daffodil?

Now you can see just how rich our so-called everyday life is if we slow down and notice. Great writers do this.

You can see just how rich life is when we notice. You'll also see how you can use this type of descriptive writing in any sort of writing you do. You can use sensory descriptions in poems, fictional stories, gratitude journals, goals and plans, journals, memoirs or letters or any other type of writing.

Exercise: Quiet Time

Walk or drive somewhere quiet. Take with you a pen and book to write in. Focus on finding somewhere very quiet outside of the familiarity of your home. If you go to a park or a beach, find somewhere away from people. Maybe the headland at the end of the beach or a quiet secluded spot in a parkland. Or go to a church or cathedral. Just ensure that you are as alone as you can be for a short time.

Take time to gaze at your surroundings, focus on something restful like water, leaves and branches of a tree or the beautiful architecture of a sacred building. Breathe slowly and deeply. Now write.

Quiet and solitude allows us to be with ourselves and to be more sensitive to where we are, what we're doing and how we're feeling.

This type of writing enriches our soul and spirit.

PART TWO
PRACTICE

Chapter Seven

Your Personal Myth

Unfold you own Myth

Rumi

Your Life Is Unique

Humans are storytellers and one of the most, if not *the* most fascinating stories we can tell is of our own journey through life.

Writing about our life encourages us to reflect on our life, the lives of others and life in general.

Many of us seem to have a deep inner need to know why we're alive.

We may ask questions like:

- What's the point?

- Why am I here?

- What have I achieved?

- What is my purpose?

- What is the meaning of life? Of my life?

Sometimes this questioning is triggered by a crisis like a life threatening illness, an accident, loss of a loved one, a relationship or a job. This type of crisis throws us into a state of mind we're not used to, one in which we may start to reflect. We try to make sense of it all.

At other times these types of questions rise up as we reach a certain stage of life. We've lived for a number of decades and had many experiences and relationships and we've learned a lot just by living. Writing about our lives is a way of not only reflecting on life but exploring its meaning further.

We don't have to write our entire life story we can just choose whatever part of our life we want to write about and reflect on. Whichever part of our life we're drawn to probably holds something precious for us to explore, so go with that flow.

Connecting With Our Roots

We are a product of our history. Although we exist in the present and we are moving to the future with every moment, part of us is our history. It's part of who we are. However we can get stuck if we spend too much time and energy in our past. Denying our history usually doesn't work because denied parts can haunt us. How often have you read the phrase *haunted by memories*. These memories lurk in the shadows but if they are brought into the light we can see them, face them, re-connect with them and know them again.

When someone comes from an abusive background or has had trauma they often disconnect to survive because to connect with the trauma is too painful. This can protect or even save them at the time but later in life these memories may resurface.

Disconnecting or ignoring or pushing down parts of ourselves doesn't have to be about abuse.

My Story

I emigrated to Australia from England in the 1970's and wanted to focus on my new life in my new country. For years I didn't feel I wanted to go back to England. After about 15 years however, I started to feel homesick. It crept into my consciousness almost imperceptibly and once there I tried to ignore it.

I didn't have the money at that time to return as we had a young family and we were building a home so I pushed it away. But whenever I watched television programs set in England I'd be left feeling deeply sad that I hadn't seen these once familiar places for so very long. I so wanted to go back. Then I would snap out of this mood and get on with my life.

As the homesickness grew it lurked in the shadows unacknowledged. It oozed into my life as dissatisfaction, boredom, and restlessness. I felt unsettled and unhappy. I continued to ignore it and excuse it away with practical reasons why I didn't need to return but it would not let me go.

After three more years and 18 years away, I could push down my feeling no longer and I returned. It was the most deeply emotional and soulful journey I have ever undertaken. My entire childhood and adolescence flooded back to me in both a sensory and spiritual lived experience of reconnection. The whole first half of my life returned to me as if it had been lost somewhere. After that initial return, my reconnection ignited, my memories enlivened I've returned many many times and re-established a deeply connected relationship with the country of my birth and younger life.

So what does reconnection do? It allows us to reclaim a lost part of who we are, it works to reintegrate that part, it makes us more whole, it helps us feel more complete – it unearths the buried treasure of memories and lived past experiences and allows us to start to feel whole.

What Do We Mean By A Personal Myth?

A myth is a story that gives meaning to life and explains why things are the way they are. Myth comes from the word 'mythos' meaning word or tale.

Our own personal myth is our own story that gives meaning to our lives and attempts to explain why it has taken the path it has taken. Myths are neither good nor bad, true nor untrue - they just are. Your own personal myth - your story - may challenge your family's myth and that of your culture. It reflects how you and only you, with your unique experience, understand your life. It's more than just recording a string of facts about yourself. It is about diving deeper and looking at the layers of your life and how they interweave and what they mean to you and only you.

Tell Me A Story

From early childhood stories are important to us. Parents read stories to children. Movies and books tell stories to audiences of millions. From childhood on, stories teach us about life just from hearing about and watching the experience of others.

Joseph Campbell spent his life studying myths around the world. He concluded that humans tell stories to connect themselves with life. He also discovered that there were similarities between the myths of cultures all over the world.

For example, he found that many myths tell of a transformation often involving a death and a rebirth. The myth often tells of a death but in our own lives the death can be the death of our old self and a rebirth of a new, more mature self. This can happen several times during a lifetime.

Ancient myths have themes that still have powerful messages today. Myths can help us get in touch with alternative ways of seeing our lives and our world. So if we work to create our own myth by writing our story in our own way we can start to see our life and our world in a new light.

Even though each of our lives is a unique and fascinating story, when we look beneath the surface, in essence, we are all similar. We all know this somewhere intuitively, that the major events of life: birth, growing up, love, loss, growing older and death are, and always have been, shared by every single one of us. They are universal experiences.

This connection with every other person who lives or who has ever lived is part of what makes our lives satisfying and meaningful.

One of the ways we can link our lives with the bigger picture of humanity is to tell our stories. How often has someone been telling you their story and you have a similar story in you somewhere? Are you ever surprised at just how similar your life experience is to someone else's even though the details are so different?

So What Is A Story?

So, what are stories anyway? What is a story?

According to the Concise Oxford Dictionary a story is *a piece of narrative...told or printed in prose or verse of actual or fictitious events, legend, myth, anecdote, novel, romance...*

A story is not just a telling of unrelated events, a story has a pattern to it which has meaning for us. A story hangs together and when we can find our individual story then our life seems more meaningful.

A life story is not just a recording of events, it also includes the *effects* of what happened and the reason that those things happened in the first place. Writing about our life can mean:

- Writing about the past the present and/or the future.

- It can be as structured as a detailed autobiography or

- As fleeting as a few lines of poetry

- Ideas about the future

- Journal entries for a day or

- Reflections on the state of the world

Your Unique Story

There are many reasons why we write about our lives.

We might want to :

- Make sense of our life

- Heal from a trauma or tragedy

- Share our life's philosophy

- Share with others what it was like living in the times we have lived

- Share with others what it was like living in the places we have lived

- Leave a record of our life for our children

- Celebrate our life in writing

- Offer other people hope and inspiration

- Make people laugh at the absurdity and the fun of life

- Raise awareness about an important issue

- Help others by sharing our story

- Tell our story in our own way

You may not be able to say or put into words *why* you want to write about your life, you just know you want to or have to. We don't have to have a reason beyond wanting to do it. However, it often has to do with meaning.

Psychiatrist Victor Frankl wrote his profoundly moving book, *Man's Search for Meaning* about his time in a Nazi concentration camp. Not only did he write a shocking and deeply moving story about the experiences of the prisoners but he also wrote about how he was able to still somehow find meaning in what seemed like the worst possible situation a human being could endure. Out of that experience he developed Logotherapy, a psychotherapy based on helping people to find meaning in life. Writing about our life can be a powerful way to find meaning.

Writing your life story can also be an effective and powerful way to challenge stereotypes and assumptions and raise awareness and push for change by sharing your actual lived experience. This is where we see a personal story and its link to our universal experiences in action. One person's story can change the perception of a whole community or more because readers are moved by a person's story, a person they usually don't know and will never meet.

Why Myths Matter

Psychotherapist Rollo May proposed that many of the psychological problems and feelings of confusion we see today are related to our culture not having strong myths to teach, sustain and inspire us.

May explains that myths use symbols to unite our conscious and unconscious minds, historical and present time and individuals with their society. Symbols transcend individual experience and speak to most people about things deeper like eternity, beauty, love, sacredness, enchantment and mystery.

So myths connect us with the mysteries of life and the very deepest parts of ourselves, our essence - parts of ourselves that can so easily get lost in our contemporary world of speed, busyness and technology.

Spiritual writer, Thomas Mann says that our modern society has lost much its connection to enchantment and the sacred. He says we need to infuse our daily lives with enchantment and the sacred to reconnect to our souls.

Myths deal with eternal truths and speak to our soul - they tell us truths about the world that never change they help us to understand life.

Myths help us to understand things like:

- A Sense of personal identity - Who am I?

- A Sense of community - Where do I belong?

- What is the purpose of my life?

- Our values

- Our way of dealing with the mysteries of birth, death, love, life and the universe.

Exploring our lives means seeing life as more than just a series of events or incidents and instead we look for patterns that give our life shape, depth and meaning.

A Life Of Feeling

The fact that we all feel, we all have emotions, means that no matter how different our outer lives are we all experience life through our senses and our emotions. We all feel, at some stage, happy, sad, confused, fearful, angry, satisfied, loving, lonely, sexy, tired, energetic, apprehensive, courageous, creative, excited and the list goes on.

The difference between us is that our different life experiences trigger different feelings at different times but as we all share these feelings in common we can relate to another person experiencing those feelings even if we're not, at that time.

Although we all share these feelings, our own lives are unique - no one else has had or will **ever** have the combination of experiences and feelings that we have had.

Writing about our life in way that speaks to the heart of others means being conscious of our lives and feelings. It means being reflective and being honest. That's not the same as sharing everything. Most of us have our private chambers under lock and key. We have our boundaries - parts of us we to share and parts of us we don't.

Having control over what we share allows us to feel comfortable and safe. But the parts of our lives that we want to share we can share honestly and openly. We can reflect on what an incident or relationship taught us, where it led us and how it changed us. Others will then connect with our story.

Chapter Eight

Journal Writing

Fill your paper with the breathings of your own heart

William Wordsworth

A Powerful Practice

Journal writing is one of the simplest, most ancient and powerful ways we can use writing to enrich our lives and discover, on a deeply personal level, who we really are. Journaling also lets us follow our life journey as we change and develop through the years. Journaling is therapeutic but it can also be joyful and creative. A place to try out ideas, unrestricted by judgment, a place to play and a place to celebrate.

Journaling records our *in the moment* thoughts and feelings and if we do this regularly, wonderful things start to happen. It is uniquely personal. The relationship between your journal and yourself cannot be replicated. It will also change over time in a uniquely personal way. That, to me, makes personal journals something much more out of the ordinary, much more special than we give them credit for. They are precious recordings that cannot ever be recaptured. A moment, a day can never be repeated so why not capture its fleeting beauty, wisdom or challenges?

Journaling is so powerful that it's almost magical! We see into the inner workings of our lives. We start to sense patterns in our lives, our thoughts, our experiences that just aren't discernible during our daily lives.

Have you ever read through your past journals and been amazed, moved, embarrassed or touched by what you've written in the past? This is a deeply personal record of your life and how you've changed over time to become who you are. That's magic.

A Family Story

Our family has a precious handwritten journal from the 1800's penned by a family member who came out to Tasmania from England. It is a fascinating and revealing personal and historical account of that person's life. It is truly remarkable and I don't think anyone could read it without being deeply moved. This man is pouring out his innermost thoughts about his life, his family, his fortune and his faith, in Tasmania, in the 1800's and we are reading it today in the 21st century!

This above all: To thine own self be true, and it must follow as the night follows the day.

Polonius in Hamlet

Journaling can be literally life changing. The simple act of recording and reflecting on our days can help us to:

- Release feelings

- 'Talk' to ourselves on the page

- Clarify our goals, explore options and make decisions

- Understand relationships

- Increase self awareness

- Rehearse how we might act or what we might say

- Decide what's really important and focus on it

- Find creative solutions

- Gain clarity and calmness in times of crisis

- Discover our life path, our passion, our purpose

- Gain perspective on our life

- ★ Free up our imagination

- Develop a writing practice

- Give voice to our innermost thoughts

- Record and explore our dreams

- Understand contradictions and ambiguities

- Deepen our gratitude

- Celebrate and savor life

- Explore and reflect on our spirituality

- And anything else we want it to be

Journal writing is probably more important now than ever before – we are super-connected these days but we often lack time and space to really be with ourselves. The internet, mobile phone, email, social media etc all connect us with others but what about authentically connecting with ourselves?

Research has shown that there are two types of thinking:

1. Practical, rational and organized

2. Imaginative, creative, poetic

In Chapter Four I talked about the two sides of the brain and how they tend to work differently. The left hemisphere functions focus on problem solving and right hemisphere functions focus on imagining and creating. When we journal - because it is free ranging - we can move from left hemisphere thinking to right hemisphere thinking without restriction.

Expressing ourselves in both these ways helps lead us to a more balanced life. It becomes a process of inner strengthening through integrating and expressing the various part of ourselves.

The renowned journal keeper, Anais Nin, wrote:

"A journal - an inner life, cultivated, nourished, is a well of strength - the inner structure we need to resist outer catastrophe and error and injustices."

Journal Choices:

Of course the most important part of journaling is the writing. But it can help us get into the flow if we think also about how we prefer to do our journaling:

- Lined or blank pages? One's not better than the other. Whichever you prefer.

- How do I choose a journal? Let the journal 'choose' you. Look at a range then choose one for no particular reason other than you chose that one.

- Pen or Keyboard? Again, whichever you prefer. There is no better way.

- Handwriting does have that physical connection between hand and brain which slows us down and grounds us. Our handwriting is unique to us and changes whereas computer print doesn't, but choose whichever you prefer.

- Special pen? This is recommended because, as humans, we attach emotional significance and meaning to things. It's what we do. Like a journal itself, a particular pen that we really like will become our *Journaling Pen* and this increases the significance of our journaling as a practice.

So How Do I Journal?

Any way you want! That's the joy of journaling. It's loose and rule-free.

In Chapter Two we explored freewriting and a journal is where we can let our freewriting have free rein. We can roam our imagination, loosen up our curiosity and creativity and be real and raw. We can pour our heart onto the page, we can celebrate and be creative and crazy.

However, if you use the ideas and techniques in this book, you will write a rich and reflective journal full of detail and meaning.

If you wish you can include:

- Factual detail to bring back memories when you read your journal

- Sensual detail to relive that memory (if you wish to relive it)

- Thoughts and feelings

- Creative play to expand your memories, thoughts and ideas

Remember it's your journal - a private precious place to be free to write as little or as much as you wish.

Ideas For Journaling:

- Write freely and spontaneously!

- Don't be concerned about spelling, grammar, neatness or even about writing full sentences. You may just write single words.

- Write any way you wish - large or small, up the page, down the page, diagonally it doesn't matter

- Include sketches, doodles, cartoons, quotes, pictures, whatever. This is all part of journaling.

- Explore and include poems, prose and stories

- Writing every day can help stop procrastination and form a routine which then makes it easier to do.

- Try to write truthfully and honestly.

*This is not about discovering **the** truth, it's about discovering **our** truth.*

- What we *really* believe in (rather than what society, family, church, media friends, say you should believe in)

- What you *really* have a passion for, love, care about, would like to do

- What you *really* dislike, are bored with, don't want to do anymore

- What you'd *really* love to do with your life

Journaling With Faith

We can ask for help, inspiration, ideas, courage, healing - whatever - using our journal. Because our mind (especially our subconscious mind) works in mysterious ways, we often find that asking a question about our life sets in train a process that leads to an answer.

If we ask a question while journaling, then we try to be patient and let that question sit, often an answer will emerge apparently from nowhere. We're not sure where it has come from: our subconscious mind? The Universe? God? Intuition? Higher Power?

It doesn't matter where we think it came from, it just *does* happen. Questions are asked and the answers arrive.

This takes faith - belief that from somewhere inside us, from a Higher Power, God, Intuition or the Universe the right answer for us at this time in our life will come.

Journaling allows us to sit with that. We can write about how difficult we might find it to have that faith, about our impatience and our doubt or our fear. But we can still sit with that faith until our answer comes. To be able to hear or sense that answer when it arrives we need space away from the bustle of daily life. Journaling time is the time when we create a space for that to happen.

Often when people doubt that the answer will come, they in fact, do get, or have, the answer but they are so distracted by the noise and demands of daily life that they can't sense or hear their *still small voice* whispering the answer to them. It doesn't yell - if often only barely whispers. We need to give it space to speak and ourselves space to listen.

Recording our Dreams

We all dream. Dreams are a part of us. Mysterious yet powerful.

When you dream - write what you recall in your journal. In detail. Also recall how you felt. Resist the urge to try and interpret. Just record. But if you *sense* what the dream means to you. Write about that.

Dreams may also carry a message which is the answer to a question. Those answers we are waiting for may come in a way that's not as obvious as a formed thought or solution. The answer may come as an intuitive hunch, an idea that won't let us go or in a dream.

Chapter Nine

The Healing Power of Writing

The wound is the place where the light enters you

Rumi

The Healing Power Of Writing

During times of personal and community trauma or sadness people write. When we go through a personal tragedy, trauma, loss or upheaval many of us write - journals, stories, poems. Some write their first poem during one of these times. After the September 11 World Trade Centre crisis many many people wrote spontaneous poetry. During war, combat troops and civilians write. Anne Frank's diary is just one example.

US Professor, James Pennebaker is a leader in the field of research showing that writing about emotional topics helps us to reduce stress, find meaning and even improve our immune system. Up to a year after doing the writing, he found the benefits were still there.

Another study by Baikie and Wilhelm found the long term benefits of expressive writing included:

- Improved immune system
- Reduced blood pressure
- Improved lung and liver function
- Less days in hospital
- Increased positive feelings
- Reduced sick days off work
- Better memory
- Improved sporting performance
- Less stress related visits to the doctor

At first the researchers thought that all these positive benefits came from the release of feelings. When they investigated further they found that it's actually more to do with the fact that people who did this writing were creating a meaningful story - they were processing events in their lives and making sense of them through writing.

The researchers also found that the people whose health improved most from doing this kind of writing used more *positive-emotion* words like love, happy, content, successful etc as well as words like understand, realize and because. Using these words showed that the writing was helping these people to make sense of their lives and their pain and to feel more optimistic.

So the creation of meaning and meaningful stories was key. Healing has a lot to do with storytelling. We can write stories about ourselves, we can re-write stories about ourselves, we can write stories about others. These stories can be factual or fictional. Whatever form they take they build a relationship within us. A relationship with ourselves in our own way. They create our biography - what we believe about ourselves and what we believe about ourselves creates our reality.

Writing lets us heal at our own pace in our own way. The fact that we have total control over our writing allows us to:

- Relive

- Reconstruct

- Rewrite

- Re-story

- Restore

- Reclaim

- Rebuild

our lives in a direct and powerful way. I believe that the direct relationship between the writer and page without anyone or anything coming between those two is one of the reasons for the power of writing to be able to heal.

People have known this intuitively since earliest times. Private thoughts have been put into countless journals for countless generations. Self-therapy is nothing new.

When I worked as a counselor with children who'd suffered sexual abuse many of my clients found it immensely helpful to write a journal. None of these clients intended to write their life stories as such rather, they wanted to draw out memories and feelings they had stored inside them and try to make some sense out of the traumatic situations they'd lived through.

One young girl wrote poems for the whole three years that I met with her. As she wrote more and more poems she was able to make some sense out of the traumatic times she was going through. She also found her own voice. She wrote poems about her family, her thoughts, people in foster homes, pets, boys, music - whatever she wanted to write about.

The 4-day writing retreats I facilitated also convinced me of the deep and healing power of writing to both transform lives. When a group of people gather together with a shared connection to writing and they are given space and time in a totally supportive environment then healing can start to happen.

Writing Wrongs

There is no 'right time' to write about the pain in your life. There is only 'your time.' Writing lets you heal in your own way at your own pace in your own style. It's not a quick fix - it lets you go through the healing process for as long as you want to and you and journaling will leave you with a beautiful, personal record of your journey.

With painful parts of life it is often said people want to find 'closure' but it's also thought that with painful aspects of life it's more about integration than closure. We weave our lives together so that the past is still there but it becomes part of the rich tapestry of our unique life. The past is not closed but it's not defining us in the present or stopping us from developing a beautiful future.

For some of us closure might feel better - like that part of our life has closed and we now focus forward on the rest of our life. There are so many ways for us to live our lives and deal with its challenges. There is never one right way.

Painful memories don't need to be banished. If someone close to us has died that will always be a part of our life. We loved them and then they were gone. But the memories, painful as they may be, can be integrated as a tender and beautiful part of us that make us more fully human but also someone who can live in the present and enjoy life and plan a future at the same time as having that painful memory gently woven into it.

Journaling To Release

Often journaling will be a way to release hurts, explore issues, vent anger etc This gives us a sense of immediate relief and that can be really helpful. Sometimes when we do this it is enough just to dump all that hurt and anger somewhere and offload the feelings. At other times it will feel right to go back and reflect on what we've written. When we read over again what we've written we'll often have insights or see situations in a new way.

This offloading of immediate feelings is one way that journaling is therapeutic but there is so much more we can do with journaling to help understand and reflect on those feelings - new perspectives, different ways of seeing a situation and forgiveness can come from reflecting on our writing.

Our Own Truth

One of, if not the most important part, of writing is that we can tell our own truth and record it. A lot of people who've gone through trauma have been silenced or felt they could not bear to share their story. Some stories are so traumatic they are buried deep or seem forgotten. When we write we start to uncover these parts of ourselves that are missing and we can start to feel more whole.

So How Do I Do This?

Writing to heal is done in exactly the same way as all the writing we've covered up to now. We use freewriting, journaling, our creativity, our inner artist and our writer's voice. Using all these techniques allows us to free up our inner resources to be able to explore those parts of us that want to heal in the most creative and nurturing way.

What is particularly important with writing for healing is that we take extra care of ourselves. This can be very challenging work and very tiring. It may bring up other parts of us that need healing. We may dream more often and more powerfully.

Take Care And Stay Safe

Some of the hurts inside us can be so deep and so painful that it feels like it's too much to cope with them on our own. It's vital that when we write about sad or painful experiences and feelings, we feel safe to do so. If they are so powerful that you feel very distressed then stop writing, get up and get back in touch with everyday life.

Then it may be important for you to share them with a professional counselor or therapist. It may be better to write them in the company of someone you trust. Someone who will keep you safe but not interfere with your writing process. Don't ever push yourself to write about things that make you feel so upset that you feel overcome by your emotions.

If we force ourselves to write about something painful because we think we should or we think it's good for us then we're just hurting ourselves over again - the last thing we need to do. We need to be kind and gentle with ourselves and write when we feel we want to - not when we feel we 'should.' Shedding tears is fine as long as we still feel able to write and not overwhelmed or too distressed.

Healing can be slow and challenging sometimes but it doesn't have to be done alone and it doesn't have to be hurried. Writing alone suits some of us and not others. Writing can feel right at one time and not at another. Always do whatever feels right and feels safe.

There Are Many Ways

Many different therapies use writing as a healing practice:

- Journal Therapy and Therapeutic Writing use journaling and personal writing

- Narrative therapy uses narrative and stories

- Poetry Therapy uses writing, poetry and stories in the healing process

- Bibliotherapy uses existing books and literature

Using Writing To Move Forward After A Challenge

When using writing to move on with your life, remember:

- You have coped and you can cope.

- To write your story of *how* you've transformed. Don't just stay with the feelings. Include what you've learned about life, about your skills, etc.

- To write about what you feel you need to do or would like to do to clear up anything left form this situation and how you want to do that and by when.

- Regroup - forgive yourself and others and nurture yourself (both these are crucial) as you move forward.

- Refocus - review your big picture, recommit to your values and your purpose and to moving forward

The apparently simple act of writing can deeply transform our lives. It can begin to release us from old hurts and allow us to forgive and move forward to re-store, restory and re-create a richer freer life.

Chapter Ten

The Good Life

Gratitude is the heart's memory.

French proverb

Gratitude, Savoring And Celebration

How do we live a happy life when our lives have such ups and downs and things can come at us so unexpectedly? We can't control other people's beliefs, behavior or emotions, we can't control world events or the weather or the economy etc etc So how do we do it? What we can do is try to live a happy life *despite* all its up and downs, twists and turns and in and outs. We try to live a happy life *anyway*.

How do we do that?

Here are three simple, proven ways that can be done easily, quickly and daily that have the power to change the way we see our lives.

They are:

1. Gratitude

2. Savoring

3. Celebration

This works well if we write about all three daily in a journal. It can be the journal you use for all our journaling but I like to have a special gratitude, savoring and celebration journal where I just record these things and nothing else.

If we pick up any book about spiritual practices it will most likely teach that gratitude is fundamental to a happy life. Having an *attitude of gratitude* has been proven to have the power to change our lives.

Gratitude

The French proverb at the start of this chapter reminds us so poetically that, *Gratitude is the heart's memory*. It belongs to the heart. Gratitude is such a beautiful, life-affirming idea and it's so easy to do.

Each day, if possible, we write the first three things that come to mind that we are grateful for.

Even if life is tough or we've had a bad day there will usually be something or someone we are grateful for. It could be a kind smile, the gentle breeze, the walk with your dog. If we find it hard because life is so challenging then it is at these very times that gratitude, savoring and celebration can be their most healing.

Studies show that writing down three things that we are grateful for on a daily basis can change our outlook, our mood and can anchor us in a calmer, more positive state.

For example, if something really difficult is happening, like someone we love is really ill then we could be grateful that we could be by their side, grateful that we live where there is good medical care, grateful for the kind nurse on night duty. These are not small things and it is never about diminishing the real traumas, strains and difficulties we can be dealing with. It is about acknowledging what is still good - human kindness, the beauty of nature, the love of children, the companionship of pets.

Gratitude is the fairest blossom which springs from the soul
Henry Ward Beecher

When life is going well we can choose to focus on how grateful we are for the things, people, opportunities etc that enable our life to be good. There may be many things we feel grateful for so we can just choose the three that come to mind first without much thought.

Savoring

Savoring means appreciating in detail. It sounds the same as gratitude but to me it's gratitude in more depth and detail.

After you've written three things you're grateful for, take each one and write a short paragraph (or as much as you like) and *really* savor those things. Describe what it is or who it is or what they did or said in minute detail using all the senses. Write it in such a way that when it's re-read it takes you straight back to that beautiful moment, that loving gesture, that glorious sunset, that delicious cake. Make your writing as detailed as possible - relish in the details of that fragment of life and the preciousness of it.

Exercise:

Try this savoring exercise that my co-facilitator, Lucy Palmer created and that we used with participants in our retreats - they loved it!

Have in front of you a piece of your very favorite chocolate or treat food of some kind. It must be one you really love.

Place it in your mouth and close your eyes. Slowly let this delectable sweet treat melt in your mouth. Concentrate on the feel and taste and sheer delight of this simple act of pleasure. When it has melted, swallow it and open your eyes.

Now write in your journal in the minutest detail what you just experienced.

Describe:

- The taste
- The feel of the treat melting in your mouth
- Your feelings as this happens
- What you did with your body as you savored it
- What it is that makes it so delicious, so pleasurable

When we savor we start to experience the world with new eyes and in new ways. We live creatively. The next step is to capture the essence of these deepened moments so that they're not lost as they surely will be otherwise. One way to do this is to write about them in whatever way we want. In our own creative way.

This can be the smallest things. A raindrop on a leaf. The way someone's hair was blowing in the wind. The smell of the fresh apples in the fruit shop today. Notice. Savor. Keep and then record these everyday treasures in whatever words come to you.

This is the joy of savoring.

Celebration

Next we can celebrate the things we are grateful for and the things we savor. We can celebrate our little wins and our big wins, the deep things and the everyday fun or frivolous things. We can just celebrate! Whenever and wherever.

As time passes and we fill our journals with gratitude and savoring and we celebrate something every day, an inner shift will gradually happen. We don't usually notice this because it's subtle but it happens. As we pay attention and give thanks and celebrate the beauty, joy and abundance in our lives no matter what is happening around us it will start to allow us to feel more in balance, more at ease and more in flow with the flow of life.

Consciousness, Awareness And Mindfulness

What we're doing here is becoming more conscious, more aware and more mindful of what is good in our lives. According to spiritual teaching if we are grateful and give thanks, more abundance will flow into our lives. Gratitude and thanksgiving are a key part of religious and spiritual teachings.

Gratitude comes from consciousness, awareness and mindfulness. To be grateful, savor and celebrate we have to first notice and be mindful of what there is to be grateful for, to appreciate, to celebrate.

Petrea King from *Quest for Life Foundation* reminds us that we need to 'fluff ourselves up' so that we feel good. She asks how, if we don't feel good ourselves, can we expect to support and nurture others? We need to nurture our bodies, minds and spirits through our five senses.

We:

- See - what beautiful things do you love to look at?

- Hear - what sounds make you feel happy and relaxed?

- Smell - what are your favorite scents?

- Touch - what do you love the feel of?

- Taste - yum - what do you love to eat?

Each day write down what you saw that was beautiful, what you smelt, what you touched, what you heard, what you tasted that brought you joy, pleasure or contentment.

If any area is lacking this is the way to notice and record that. Then we can do something about it. If you find there are days and days going by where you never record a beautiful scent then record how you will do something about this. Will you buy a bottle of essential oil or body lotion? A freshly bakes loaf of bread? A bunch of flowers? Walk by the ocean and breathe deeply?

It's quite easy to bring more joy and contentment into our lives by being mindful of our senses, noticing what we lack and bringing some of those things into our daily lives.

Chapter Eleven

Dare to Dream

Go Confidently in the Direction of Your Dreams! Live the Life You've Imagined
Thoreau

Discover Your True Purpose Through Writing

Exercise:

What are my deepest values?

Merriam-Webster dictionary defines a value as: *something (such as a principle or quality) intrinsically valuable or desirable*

We live our lives according to our values whether we know it or not. Everything from:

- Our choice of partner and friends
- Where we live

- What occupation we have
- Whether we have children or not
- What we spend our spare time doing
- Where we go on holiday
- Which charity we donate to
- What we choose to buy

These are all intimately tied to our values though we often don't realize it.

Read the list of values below. Please add more values to the list to make it your own. Now choose about five of these that feel like they are the most important in your life.

- Achievement

- Adventure

- Authenticity

- Beauty

- Being the best

- Challenge

- Comfort

- Compassion

- Courage
- Creativity
- Curiosity
- Education
- Empowerment
- Environment
- Family
- Freedom
- Financial abundance
- Fitness
- Friendship
- Giving service
- Health
- Honesty
- Independence
- Inner peace
- Integrity
- Intelligence
- Intimacy

- Kindness

- Joy

- Justice

- Leadership

- Learning

- Love

- Passion

- Peace

- Personal Growth

- Personal empowerment

- Play

- Productivity

- Quiet

- Relationships

- Respect

- Security

- Sexuality

- Solitude

- Spirituality

- Success

- Variety

- Wealth

- Wisdom

- Work

Now see if you can order them 1 - 5 with 1 as the most important value in your life right now. Your preferences may have changed over time but do it as of now.

What do these five values and the order you have placed them in tell you about?

- Your life so far

- Your life now

- Your life in the future

Now write your number one value in big letters in the centre of a blank page in your journal. Write the other four value words scattered around the rest of the page in smaller letters. Leave the rest of the page blank. Look at these words. Then take a blank fresh journal page and write for five minutes on each word ending with writing for five minutes about your main value word.

- What did you write about?

- What did it reveal to you?

- Are you surprised by anything?

- Did you have any insights?

- What intrigued you about what you wrote?

- How could what you wrote help you in crafting your life right now and in the future?

The more clarity we have around our deepest values, the more we can create a future that is meaningful, joyful, soulful and truly ours.

We need to not be concerned if our life up to now has not matched with our values as much as we wish it had. For many of us it may not have. But everything we've done in life has been precious and valuable and has been directing us more and more towards what our unique life is really about.

To truly refine what we want to create in our future it helps to ask ourselves questions that both open us up to possibilities and clarify more what we already know.

Questions To Help Us Dare To Dream

Daring to dream allows us to explore the possibilities out there waiting for us, it allows us to take stock and remind ourselves of what we dreamed of in the past for our lives and what we dream of now.

Answer these questions:

- What makes you smile? (Activities, people, events, hobbies, projects, etc.)

- What were your favorite things to do in the past? What about now?

- What activities make you lose track of time?

- What makes you feel great about yourself?

- Which ten people inspire you most? (Anyone you know or do not know. Living or not.)

- What qualities inspire you, in each person you chose?

- What do people typically ask you for help with?

- If you could choose to teach something, what would it be?

117

- What will you regret not doing, being or having in your life?

- What could you devote your life to if you were free to?

- If you could live anywhere, where would you live?

- What are you naturally good at and love to do?

- What comes easily to you? (Skills, abilities, gifts etc.)

- What have you never done that you've always wanted to do?

Exercise:

Designing The Future

Our Personal Vision Statement

Creating and writing A Personal Vision Statement for our life means taking the time to focus on how we want our life to look and how we want to feel. This is key to creating a meaningful future. If we don't create our future it will then just happen and we may end up wondering why we're not living a more satisfying life.

A Personal Vision Statement that works is one that inspires and uplifts us when we read it and one that is clear and focused.

To give our life meaning and purpose it's important to have a vision that:

- Inspires and expands us beyond our everyday activities

- Excites us when we think about it

- Resonates with something deep within us

- Is bigger than us

- Is aligned with our values

- Feels like a challenge

- Gives our life purpose and deep meaning

Exercise:

Looking Back

Imagine you are now 90 years old, sitting in your very favorite place; you feel blissful and happy, you are pleased with the wonderful life you've lived. It's had its up and downs, its good times and its difficult times but looking back at what you've achieved and experienced, all the relationships you've had, all the places you've been you feel deeply satisfied.

Still imagining yourself at 90 years old, write down your answers to the following:

- What has mattered to you most?

- What have you done or created that you feel the most satisfied about and why?

- What made your life the happiest?

- What was your greatest challenge and how did you overcome it?

- What is one thing you wish you'd done differently?

- Who were the people who meant the most to you in your life?

- What made your life uniquely yours?

- What gave your life deep meaning?

- What did you enjoy the most?

Now take each one and write a paragraph thinking about the following:

- What does this tell you about your life now and in the future?

- What does this tell you about your deepest values?

Read through what you've written.

Now take some time to compose your Personal Vision Statement. It can be as short or as long as you need it to be.

How To Word A Personal Vision Statement

There is no right or wrong way to write a Personal Vision Statement but usually they are worded like a commitment to what you vision for your ideal life that is in line with your values.

It is often a series of statements about how we will live our lives. It often covers the various areas of life such as family, work, community and faith.

The statements may start with phrases like:

- I commit to…

- I will be a person who…

- I will use my gifts to…

- I will conduct myself in such a way as to…

- I will live each day as…

- What I will achieve in my life…

- I will create…

- I will use my life to...

Avoid going into the details of *how* you will do what you state. Your goals are the how-to's for achieving what you put forward in your Personal Vision Statement.

Write your Personal Vision Statement out in statements - then rewrite it until it feels right. For now. It can change. It can be refined.

If you want to - use pens, textas, paint, whatever you like and create a poster of your statement. Decorate it if that feels right.

Writing is a truly powerful way to turn our Personal Vision Statement into our Personal Vision. Some people love to do collage Vision Boards which is a pictorial way to display a Vision Statement.
Choose whichever way you want to create your Personal Vision Statement.

Others prefer to concentrate on just writing out the Statement and leaving it unadorned.

Whichever you choose, you can then either display it so you see it regularly or roll it up like a scroll. If you keep it rolled up then have a ritual of unrolling it like an ancient scroll and reading it regularly.

The important thing is to create a Personal Vision Statement right now so that the opportunity does not pass by. Writing it down will create subtle changes in your mind. It will focus you. It will help you be more aware of what matters to you and what you want to do with your future.

As your Personal Vision Statement starts to take shape you may find that you can already sense a stirring inside. You start to realize there are things that you *really* want to do in the future. Your Statement helps you see this in front of you, in writing.

Your subconscious mind will then start working on ideas to make this happen and opportunities and resources may start to come to you seemingly from nowhere.

Read your Personal Vision Statement very regularly to keep the ideas planted in your consciousness where they will take root and flourish.

Change

Life changes. Every second of every day, life changes.

The weather changes, our body changes, our moods and thoughts change, events happen, things, grow, things die, there is birth, there is death, there is decay, there is creation, there is movement.

We can feel unnerved and unsettled sometimes by this constant changing world. Some of us spend untold amounts of time, energy and money trying to stop or slow down change.

Trying to stop change can cause us a lot of stress and heartache. We might try and stop change in our life by:

- Staying with relationships that no longer nurture or satisfy us,

- Staying in a career/job that bores us

- Living in places that don't fit with our lives any more

- Working harder and harder so that we don't get retrenched

- Getting further and further into debt

- Becoming increasingly worried about ageing

- Hanging on to old ideas that have had their time

We can use writing to help us create ideas and plans that, when we act on them, will help us to thrive in this world of constant and increasing change. Writing can help us feel less unnerved because we can explore and understand our reactions and feelings towards change instead of letting them build up inside us to a point where they can become worrying or even at times overwhelming which then makes us even more concerned about change.

Making It Happen

There's a lot of information around on creating change by manifesting, goal setting, intentions etc. A lot of it's good stuff and some of it's - let's just say, not so good. I do believe in manifesting because common sense tells me that what we focus on we're likely to act on and bring into being. One way to really energize an intention and create a powerful path to manifesting it, is to write it down.

Writing down our intentions and goals also helps to quieten down our inner doubter, critic, negative voice - whatever you want to call it. That tedious little recording that says things like:

- Really? You want to do that?

- Who do you think you are?

- Now how do you think you're going to do that?

- What you?

- But what about…..? (Your age, your lack of money, you inexperience etc etc etc)

Sound familiar?

Writing can help shut that annoying little creature up. If we focus on the writing and exclude everything else we can move forward despite those messages. Then our intentions are there in writing. If we capture them in words they have already started to manifest because we already have them recorded in black and white.

Writing Down Your Goals

One way we can create some order in our journey towards our Personal Vision is create and write down goals with various timeframes that all work together towards the same end:

1. Long term goals - 5 years, 2 years, 1 year.

2. Medium term goals - 6 months, 90 days, 30 days - we can break down the long term goals into smaller segments

3. Short term goals - 30 days, 2 weeks, 1 week - we can break down the medium term goals into doable pieces that are much easier to achieve but they build towards the longer term goals and towards our Personal Vision.

No matter how many times you've read about goal setting, it truly is a powerful method for achieving our Personal Vision. We are far more likely to reach our goals if we write them down and break them up into smaller chunks. Goals that stay in our heads are daydreams. To make things happen we have to materialize those goals - we need to give them form. The first step in writing them down so that:

- They are more real and not just in our head

- We are forced to be specific about what we want - we move on from vague ideas

- We can keep our written goals where we see them regularly and keep focused

- We can use our written goals as part of an action plan for success

Get Creative!

If we just write a list of our goals that might seem uninspiring.

As with our Vision Statement, we may do better if we turn our list into something more creative.

If you like doing lists and they work for you - please do lists because it's crucial we do what works for us and we're all different.

But if lists don't work well for you then start out by writing your goals in a list.

Then be still and quiet. Ask yourself *How would I like to display my goals to myself? What layout would I like?*

Some examples are:

- A simple uncluttered list

- A letter to myself

- A mind map type visual poster and putting my goals on there

- Another type of poster? With pictures like a vision board

- A document that looks like an ancient scroll

- A section of my journal with a page for each of my goals

- On cards that I can carry with me

However you'd like to display your goals is right for you. The idea is to present your goals in a way that energizes and inspires you when you look at them because then you need to....

Read what you've written **at least** twice day, every single day that you possibly can!

Best time to read them?

1. Immediately on waking before you get out of bed

2. In bed, just before you fall asleep

Why These Times?

At these two particular times of the day we are relaxed and drifting either out of or into sleep and at these times, messages we tell ourselves will much more easily drift into our subconscious where they can do their powerful work towards achieving our goals.

Advertisers and marketers are masters at understanding how to get messages into our subconscious minds where most of our decisions are **really** made.

If they spend millions doing this, it's because it works, and we can use the same method to help get our own messages, that have deep meaning for us, that are **our** messages not someone else's, into our own subconscious mind so we can get results.

Because our conscious mind is the one that appears to run the show and it operates on patterns, habits, conscious ideas, rational thought etc, we often think this is where we achieve things but the **real** work goes on in our subconscious.

Never go to sleep without a request to your subconscious

Thomas Edison

Final Thoughts

Writing down our thoughts, feelings, ideas, dreams, values, Vision Statements, goals etc allows us to find out what we *really* want for ourselves and others. In the hustle and bustle of life we often forget what it is we *really* want to do with our life. What our real passion was as a child that we may have forgotten or buried over time.

Writing can help restore our balance, recover what we really love, restore our soul and help us work towards bringing our envisioned life into form so that we live abundantly, meaningfully and creatively.

I wish you many years of fruitful musings…

The art of writing is the art of discovering what you believe

Gustav Flaubert

About The Author

Linda Robson Bell is a writer, coach, course designer, teacher and counselor. She has been writing and teaching for over twenty years. Linda has designed writing courses in creative writing, memoir journaling and therapeutic writing. Writing was one of the major cornerstones of her client work during her professional career as a counselor, social worker and therapist.

Linda gained a Masters Degree in Creative Writing from the University of Sydney and this is her second book. Linda is currently completing her first novel.

Linda was born in the decade after World War II into an extended family whose roots can be traced back to very early settlers in Britain arriving around the 7th Century BC. Many of Linda's relatives still inhabit this cold, beautiful, wild part of north-east England while Linda now lives in the sunny southern hemisphere city of Sydney.

Always an avid reader and scribbler, after two decades as a professional social worker Linda started writing seriously during mid life and completed her Creative Writing degree. Linda has had numerous short stories published while creating and teaching writing courses including a 4-day residential retreat course in Personal Writing for the Quest for Life Foundation.

Linda would love to hear from you about your writing. She runs The Wellspring Centre offering programs for writers, coaches and counselors and a gathering of writings, books and resources for those of us who write, read and ponder on life's mysterious and wondrous ways.

Find The Wellspring Centre at:

www.thewellspringcentre.com
Instagram @lindarobsonbell
Email Linda at: info@thewellspringcentre.com